Seafarer

ALSO BY JAMES LONGENBACH

POEMS

Forever

Earthling

The Iron Key

Draft of a Letter

Fleet River

Threshold

PROSE

The Lyric Now

How Poems Get Made

The Virtues of Poetry

The Art of the Poetic Line

The Resistance to Poetry

Modern Poetry after Modernism

Wallace Stevens

Stone Cottage

Modernist Poetics of History

Seafarer

///////////////////////

NEW POEMS
WITH *Earthling* AND *Forever*

James Longenbach

W. W. NORTON & COMPANY
Independent Publishers Since 1923

For information about permission to reproduce selections from
this book, write to Permissions, W. W. Norton & Company, Inc.,
500 Fifth Avenue, New York, NY 10110

For information about special discounts for bulk purchases, please
contact W. W. Norton Special Sales at specialsales@wwnorton.com
or 800-233-4830

Manufacturing by Lakeside Book Company
Book design by Lovedog Studio
Production manager: Gwen Cullen

ISBN 978-1-324-07584-4

W. W. Norton & Company, Inc., 500 Fifth Avenue,
New York, N.Y. 10110
www.wwnorton.com

W. W. Norton & Company Ltd., 15 Carlisle Street,
London W1D 3BS

1 2 3 4 5 6 7 8 9 0

for
Joanna, Kathryn, Alice, Marc

Contents

Seafarer (2022)

Now Then

Forever (2021)

I

II

III

Earthling (2017)

I

II

III

IV

Seafarer

/ / / / / / / / / / / / / /

NOW AND THEN

1. *Borough*

James is walking down Main Street,
He's putting one foot ahead
Of the other, one, two, he's watching an egret

Stepping through the reeds, its body
Startled, then
Frozen, looking for fish.

Why can't he walk like that?
Behind the old wall
That was Lynn and Jeff's house. There's

The bench where somebody's sitting every
Day but not today:
The sun's too hot or else

Not hot enough, the water clear
Enough to see minnows
Hiding in the grass.

2. Admonition

He acknowledges the sins of the people
In the wilderness, but still
He's troubled by one:

His pulse, his urine, his sweat—they all say nothing.
Neither does he find
Changes in his appetite,

His mind neither corrupted nor infatuated—
Yet his family, his friends,
They see something imperceptible,

Something always present
Which has established
An empire inside him: here

Is a certain *secret d'état* never
To be said out loud
By which he's bound.

3. *Egret*

My mother fished this spot, my father, too.
Probably you couldn't have told
Them apart, but my mother

Fledged me, then she was gone.
I heard she met a terrible end. Can I say that?
In the summer of '68 my father

Went to Newark for art supplies:
Crowds of people, open
Hydrants, shattered plate-glass—

The dent below the passenger-side
Window of the Chevy
Was left by a thrown brick: it stayed

Until the Chevy was replaced.
Of famine, love, difference
Of skin I knew nothing.

4. *First Day*

You compose yourself: *compose,*
From the Old French *composer,*
To put together, to write.

You're assigned a desk. Even now
I'm seated at a desk, I'm watching men
Fill a dumpster from an empty house: *quarantine,*

From *quaranta giorni,* the practice
Of keeping ships from entering
Venice for forty days. You never speak

Of school, you run home for lunch.
You like your egg salad
On toast, you still do; but that morning

You learned about other
Languages, you sang
A little song: *Dites moi pourquoi.*

5. *Why*

In the beginning, people
Were visible powers
Of nature, like the stars

And the moon. Nor did I believe
In God: not that we'd had
A quarrel, only that his service,

As it was described, seemed disagreeable.
The consequence was not,
As anyone might expect, that I grew

Selfish or disrespectful,
But when affection came
It came with a passion

Uncontrollable, at least
By me, who'd never
Had anything to control.

6. *Limousine*

Immediately after closing my eyes forever
I'm gliding through the borough
In a big car: there's

The Holy Ghost Society,
And down by the water
Young people, most of them wearing

Floppy hats, little else!
I'm driving down Main Street
At quarter to twelve

In the morning, the car
Stopping at a house where
Now, no older than four, maybe five,

There's little James
Still running, also
Looking around.

AFTER DINNER

1.

Beautiful this stone wall, broken
By fate, the roof collapsed, a tower
Crumbling, lichens thickened by time. Builders
Are buried in unmarked graves,
Hundreds walk past.
How the wall outlasts them, layered with moss, through one
Administration, another! Fallen, though
Pieces of it stand . . . worn . . .
On this discarded earth old thinking . . . a design
That reinforced the wall ingeniously
With iron braces. Rooms
Were bright, the roof
High, buoyed by murmurings.
Then sickness in the countryside, slaughter, too,
Fortifications breached, houses abandoned,
And people who'd fix anything
Laid in earth: here
They stood, smiling
At one another, flushed with wine,
Looking at heaps of silver
And diamonds, prosperity, wealth—at a wall
Enclosing everything,
Even our hearts: this was fitting.
Then let the water . . . pour over
These gray stones . . . until
The sea . . . then . . .

2.

The first few snowdrops, daffodils
Rising in the patch of sun.
Who planted them? Chairs

Around the dinner table,
Games we played, our leaders
Forgettable, for a moment, even

The ones with whom we never agreed—
If we recognize how oysters
Clean the bay until we

Split them, savoring the brine, still
A voice whispers, *I'll take*
Everything that's yours.

My mother's teacups?
I'll bind your arms, breach
The wall, hire a pitiless jailor—

We found a bracelet
Buried in the sand, gold star
In a mackerel's teeth—breathe

The air: it can't be difficult
To start, to stop,
A cry, a little tear—

3.

Tell it whole, sing like a god,
    As Homer said: water churned
Over the wall, littering earth
    With tree limbs, which we burned.

4.

A king once convened his advisors, asking
For thoughts on an invisible god.
When I compare our life with the endless time
Following it, said one, *I picture a sparrow*
Careening back and forth in this hall.
He waved his hand across the room.
Here, while we sopped up stew by the fire,
Snow blew hard against the window,
Inches from our faces. I was warm,
Everyone was warm! But inches
Above my head the sparrow was afraid:
In one door it flew, out another—
For decades I've repeated this story.
Probably, as old people say often,
I've known it my entire life.
Ascending the stairs my legs grew heavy,
To myself I seemed quiet as a stone,
Undemanding, busy, complete—
Imagine floating in the evening sky,
A few strays walking the street, talking quietly.
Never did the sparrow seem oblivious
To warmth: given the walls, the way
It lived, skittish, then soaring after dark,
It felt a little safer in the storm.

DORSODURO

I position my cup, my plate, a question circling, looking for home:
do you drink tea with ambrosia?

✦

Window looking at the sea, pine tree bending to the water, window looking at the street, wind lifting snow in curls.

✦

My mother smocked dresses for our daughters. One day, someone knows how to smock dresses, then nobody knows.

✦

The train is full of young people: even in winter, everyone wearing parkas, you can sense their beautiful bodies. Where are they going?

✦

My kidney's embolized, my heartbeat's strong. All we have to do, the question and I, is fall asleep. The doors are closing, hurry!

✦

The boat was ours, I didn't want to leave, all of us were there. Then it was morning, we were in Dorsoduro.

WE CAN SAY

1.

The Morandi bridge collapses in a rainstorm: *o Dio*, repeats a
man who watches it fall, *o Dio*.

The highway occupies a narrow strip of land beside the sea, it
crosses many bridges.

We follow the highway into France: a corkscrew village with a
bakery and a post office is surrounded by fields of lavender.

For a moment, the words *misi me*, Italian for *I embark*, don't
match exactly the words *je me mis*; they feel more adamant.

Until the sea closes over us again.

2.

We live in a house
With many windows.
Because everyone
Wants to swim,
There's the sea.
From the roof we see
Gardens for herbs,
Gardens for flowers—
I don't imagine
We'll live forever,
Nobody does.
My goal here
Is clarity.

3.

The San Giorgio bridge replaces the Morandi; jets trail green, white, and red smoke.

They have no idea what we're going through, says a bystander.

The waves sparkle.

It reminded me of childhood, says another, *how we drove across it for the best clothes in town.*

4.

Who lifted these stones? Everywhere I'm standing on the back
Of great labor while the ocean seethes: then newspapers
Piled on the wicker chair go sailing high as the roof.

Windowpanes shatter, exploding not in the house
But toward the street, great shards balancing in treetops
Where it's difficult to see them. Lightning, silence—

Put an ear to the floorboards you can hear water
Trickling beneath the blue house with pretty windows,
The peeling house across the street—gray, green, violet, pink,

The colors of land and water shifting. Not long ago we'd stand
Beside the Wreck, stream running into Sunset Pond.
Stone repelled water, saltmarshes restored the coastline after storms—

Beneath this sky, this quiet light, people are peering
Out of doorways, little shops. I need
Umbrellas, place mats, drawing paper, a broom, bedside lamps.

WILD LILIES

Souls gathered, some grown old, others new, bearing the clothes they'd worn. Don't leave my body lying there, said one. Plant your oar, live far from the sea, advised another. Did you suffer a long illness, asked one of us. Not really, answered my mother, only my loneliness. Then spoke Achilles, whom we'd ranked with the immortals.

> *Let's not listen to any more gossip*
> *About heaven: better to be fed*
> *After breaking the soil, a farm hand*
> *For some country man, working for bread.*

He asked about his family. We told him what we knew, then watched him running through a field of wild lilies.

—after Homer

TWO AND A HALF ODES

No gilded walls here, no beams
Carved from marble,
Columns of the rarest wood—
My father didn't leave a fortune, he was a teacher.
Dawn follows nighttime,
The new moon wants to be visible,
But it's hard to be satisfied, hard not to build
New houses cantilevered
Over the bay. We all exist at the edge
Of the grave, yet I want to own
The neighbor's cottage—mattress
Tied to the car roof,
Children waving goodbye—
And in the background always
The sound of the sea: no house waits
More patiently than the one in hell.
Son of a teacher,
Son of riches—nobody
Could rescue the son of Zeus, founder
Of the house of Atreus,
Who lives in hell forever.
He stole ambrosia from the gods, who
Summoned or not, might answer
A poor man's prayers.

✦

One of us plants more grapes,
One has a leg up
Because of his father, another, more followers—

Damocles couldn't enjoy the feast
With a sword above his head, no birdsong, no lutes,
But sleep comes quickly
To a little house
Untroubled by the sea.
The one who desires what he has—
His vineyards aren't beaten
By hail, his fruit trees never getting
Too much sun,
Then too little—
Fish know the sea is smaller
When a builder dumps a load of rubble
There, foundations for a house: land is never enough.
Palaces, yachts—
Worry sits down right
Beside the writer as he writes.
If neither marble, silk, nor wine
Can soothe me in the middle of the night,
Why should I change
This little island?

✦

I wanted
To sing of greater sorrows, the siege of cities,
But Apollo plucked his lute
Ahead of time, chiding
Me for spreading sails on the sea.

—*after Horace*

BIG AS LIFE

Travel, cookbooks, philosophy, Kant—
Also a cast of the winged lion
From a stationer east of the Arsenale,
Also a riding crop, bronze handle,

Shaft woven from eight strands
Of leather, one at the tip—
Outside, a cormorant dives
Beneath the water, a barge chugs up

The inlet, circling Sandy Point: the crop
Was carried by Loretta Kearns
Of Bridgeport, whose daughter
Maureen Howard once pondered

Art deco murals smarting up
The lobby of the Eldorado,
Ignored for years, then hobbled
To the Park, no coat, no scarf,

Up the Bridal Path, over her head
Eager-to-bloom cherry trees
Throwing black shadows
On the barest scrim of snow—

How the gold has grown dim,
How the pure gold is changed!
The sacred stones lie scattered
At the head of every street!

TIME TO GO

1. *Story*

March, clouds low as the ceiling,
I pedaled beside the cove.
Across a succession

Of ploughed fields divided by wire I saw
One living thing, a boy my age
Carrying a gun: immediately

He ran across the furrows.
I doubted he'd catch me
But when he did

He smiled, breathing heavily.
Well, I asked, *what do you want?*
I wanted to watch you go.

2. Backstory

On Christmas Eve your father dies,
The skirt you buy reversible,
One side black, the other red,

The boy you love drafted
On his eighteenth birthday.
If you wax the Chevy, scrub the screens

Each spring, laying them
On the apron of the garage,
You keep death at bay: the mind

And the hands are tuned together,
Hands moving with the mind,
Mind listening to the hands.

3. Interpretation

A boy was scaring away gulls
The old-fashioned way,
With a flintlock. *Going off half-cocked,*

A flash in the pan,
Lock, stock, and barrel!
The trigger was turned

To the half-cocked position, the flash-pan
Sprinkled with powder, the rest
Stuffed down the barrel.

Seagulls, terns, more gulls
Ripping the sown ground,
Tearing it, the water in sight—

4. *Invitation*

Climb the hill at sunset, higher,
You'll see a river of gold
Flowing from a cleft

In rock, smoke dribbling
From the chimneys
Ochre and blue. You'll see a swatch

Of unploughed land between
The rocks, headstones toppled, hard to read,
An old man dressed in evening clothes

Portioning out the turbot, slicing
The roast, then parting
His cobwebbed lips to speak.

5. Seafarer

Mæg ic be me sylfum soðgied wrecan,
Siþas secgan, hu ic geswincdagum
Earfoðhwile oft þrowade,

Bitre breostceare gebiden hæbbe,
Gecunnad in ceole cearselda fela,
Atol yþa gewealc—

I can tell a true story about myself,
Speak openly of my travels, how in long days
Often I've endured hardship,

Abided bitter heartbreak,
Known on shipboard the embrace of sorrow,
The terrible reach of waves.

6. Reality

The gun was pointed at the ground,
The boy neatly dressed.
I pedaled away. But I thought

About what he'd said really
For years: happily I'd be learning
An invention or shelling peas,

Splitting the green pods with my thumb,
And in my mind he'd appear. Voila!
But I never saw him again, neither the gun.

Was he a phantom? Did I conjure him?
Probably you've wondered
This, but was he real?

THE INTERPRETER

1.

Often he stands behind me, slightly to the left,
Like a waiter in a jacket and tie.
If I drop my napkin
He retrieves it, drapes it over my chair,
He takes away my soup plate, brings the cheese. But on this day
The interpreter of my thoughts brought
Something strange,
To which I was unaccustomed; he translated it
Into English for me. I'd ordered
Linguini tossed with tomato, penne with ham.
At lunchtime you could do that:
Half and half, you'd say,
And some days there'd be risotto, some days
Tortellini—I took my seat
Beside the window, leaned my book
Against a bottle of wine,
And though I'd taken
Only a few bites, the room
Suddenly was empty: no one
Was waiting for a check, neither was anyone
Impatient to take my place. Tables
Had been set for dinner, silverware, napkins—outside
The wind was silent.
Only when it met something
Other than itself, sand, the branches
Of a sycamore—

2.

Some people hid themselves where they ate delicate food and drank fine wine, always in moderation.

Others retreated to the countryside; they carried flowers, scented herbs, or a collection of spices.

Cows, sheep, and pigs were driven into the fields, where the wheat was left unreaped.

Houses stood empty, fortunes languished.

Without thinking, often without effort or connivance, people took what had been left behind and made something.

3.

Right above our heads
New stars are born.
New words occur
To us, whole poems.

What's a dipper? It's
A kind of spoon.
Above our heads
New stars are born.

Why live by day? In a blaze
Of sunlight everything
Above us fades.
I'll show you stars
Above your head.

4.

Another word for the interpreter,
  Sang the wind, ensuring I was fed,
Is medium, the intermediate,
  Who speaks among the living for the dead.

5.

I was reading Boccaccio's tales when a new virus was discovered in Wuhan; I hadn't finished when Kyiv was bombed.

Boccaccio wrote what Latin became in Florence. I'm writing in French and German. French: *discover, emergency.* German: *read, new.*

Keep your balance while putting your right foot in front of your left. Why keep?

I never thought I'd see this moment in my lifetime, says a woman who'd grown up in Mississippi: the legislature voted to change the state flag, removing the symbol of the Confederacy.

6.

The person I was at the beginning
Found himself at a frontier
Drawn to be erased,

Established elsewhere.
There it is, no, there.
Remember eating in a restaurant?

I remember *often he stands*, I remember
The window, its coincidence
Of the Gothic and the Moorish, the latticework—

I abandoned that restaurant quickly,
As if running away.
But I remember the window

As I might remember a person seen
Casually in the grocery store:
He might have lived

Near us, he might have felt
A degree of friendship.
Did this happen in a foreign city?

Did this happen at all? When I saw
The window many years later, I wept
Because it seemed to say

I remember your parents.
This happened quickly,
Then it took time to write it down.

NOW THEN

1. *Stars*

One island grows asparagus,
Uses only trucks with three wheels.
Boats churning up the harbor
Before dawn, chugging back at noon—
When the sun rose that day
Her body, lying beside his, was still warm.
A tear dribbled down his cheek
Slowly as he told this story,
Sitting on the grass.
Did we say good-bye,
Walk home, climb our stairs?—
Orion once boasted he could master
All the wild animals, but earth
Sent a scorpion: both
Were raised to heaven. Orion
Shows his jeweled sword in winter,
So our summer night was lit
By the stars of Scorpio.

2. Hotel Earth

Cornices overgrown with moss,
The stoop with nettles, flower beds
Hardly discernible beneath brambles and weeds—
Next door was a place where drinks
Were sold, so I ordered
A glass of red wine. *The Earth?*
For years it never changed, said the bartender.
Now kids won't come around at night.
Doors close by themselves
As if clouds were gathering, bang!
Footsteps climb the staircase, one, two—
I paid the tab. Does anything stay
There, hatred, the capacity for love?
There's the baby in a red striped sweater
Against blue sky, my left hand
Holding her, my right the camera.
She's smiling at you.
We're invisible, like the sea.

3. *Now Then*

Were these gardens spacious
As on the mainland, this
Would be the largest borough in the world.
Old people are sitting on benches,
Young people running—
What shall we do? Originally
Fishermen raised these houses
As the land allowed: together let's sing
The prettiest marriage song—
Here they are! May Leto, guardian of children,
Provide beautiful children,
Aphrodite ensure you love each other
Equally, and Zeus give you riches.
Instill in each other more
Than affection, but remember
That the rooster lifts
His neck to sing, too. We'll be
Here when the water says *I'm here.*

Forever

(2021)

/ / / / / / / / / / / / / / /

I

TWO PEOPLE

1.

Two people at the end of a dock, facing the sea, the sky.
Behind them a party, clink of glasses.
Guests still relevant to their lives
But not essential;
Parents, family friends.

Two people not yet old, but no longer young.
Before them the harbor, they're facing west, they're watching the
    sun go down.
The sky is bright, and then, remarkably, it's dark again.

They've never done this before,
They've done it a thousand times.

The sun goes down,
The stars come out,
Even the lights above the patio are beautiful.

2.

How do you imagine the shape of one lifetime?
A circle, a tangle of lines? He knows
That if he kisses her
She'll kiss him back,
But he waits, they're going to spend their lives together; he knows
   that, too.

Behind them, growing louder, the past:
The one who left, the one who would not go away—

What happens when a wish comes true?
A room by the sea, a bed, a chair.

You're a little sunburnt, a breeze, white curtains billowing,
And as you raise your arms
She lifts the tee shirt from your body.
Perfect gentleness, the perfect glint of pain.

3.

Where will we be in five years, five years after that?
This is a game they play.
Often they play it in a restaurant, Rue de L'Espoir.
A basket of bread, two round glasses of wine. How free they feel!

Five years from now I want us each to have a book.
We'll live in London, maybe Rome.

Five years from that we'll have a baby, what will we name her? She'll
    be a girl.

It all comes true—everything
They ever wished
And more, two girls.

Remember the party behind them, the voices?
They never went away.
But the sound of the sea grew louder.

NOTRE-DAME

High above our heads the forest
Is burning, oaks and chestnuts almost a thousand years old.
Smoke is rising, alarms are ringing,
But down here in the past
We're ignorant, we're unprepared.

This boy lights a candle in a little red cup.
Maybe the girl he loves
No longer loves him.
Look at her, she's standing right beside him; isn't he dumb?

This boy's going to be a father, he's just found out.
Together with his wife
He'll celebrate at Le Trumilou, their favorite bistro, just across the
    Seine.

Viollet-le-Duc is sketching a buttress.
Louis Vierne is playing Bach, the *Toccata and Fugue in D Minor.*
They're embellishers, both of them,
They can't leave the past alone! Doesn't anyone
Hear the sirens, see the black smoke
Billowing against the sky?

The forest is burning. Beneath it
Little flames of hope
Are burning, too.
Hope, desire, longing, fear—

This boy doesn't know he has cancer. This boy
Doesn't realize that, being
Who he is, he asks too much;
The people he loves need less of him.

This boy? He will live forever
In a little house by the sea.

THE WAY I LIKE BEST

Initially the fragments were discovered by Helena,
Mother of the emperor Constantine.
Where precisely, or in what circumstances,
Nobody knows for sure.
Stolen by the Persians in 614,

✦

They were recovered intact by Heraclius,
Emperor of the East, in 628.
But because the blood of Jesus had rendered the wood
Imperishable, no matter
How many pieces were removed,

✦

The fragments were divided into increasingly smaller fragments,
Each of them, because more easily concealed,
More valuable than the last.
Smuggled out of Jerusalem by two friars,
Entrusted to the Patriarch of Constantinople in 1366,

✦

Two such splinters were delivered *nel palmo*,
In the palm of the hand,
To the guardian of the Scuola Grande San Giovanni Evangelista,

One of the six Venetian *scuole* or guilds.
There, in the Oratorio della Croce,

✦

You'll find the cross-shaped reliquary in which the splinters,
Arranged to mimic
A cross, are encased in rock crystal.
You won't find the cycle of narrative paintings
Commemorating their acquisition, because in 1806, after dissolving
the *scuole*,

✦

Napoleon removed the paintings from the walls.
Gentile Bellini, Carpaccio, Perugino—
Each depicts the reliquary.
Each depicts a miracle,
Though in Bellini's *Miracle of the Merchant Jacopo de Salis*

✦

The miracle is hard to find.
Jacopo, robed in red,
The only person
Kneeling in a sea
Of white-cowled celebrants

✦

Carrying the cross to which he prays,
Is completely alone.

His son is dying,
It's the feast of San Marco,
The presentation of the true cross, April 25, 1444—

✦

To see the *Miracle of the Merchant Jacopo de Salis* properly,
As for thirty years I did not, remember that in the Scuola
It was hung above your head;
In the Accademia you'll need to kneel.
To see the reliquary of the Scuola Grande San Giovanni
      Evangelista,

✦

Start in the southwest corner of the Campo San Giacomo,
The one with the sycamores you like.
Cross the bridge, turn left, then right, then left again—
The first time I ever saw Venice
I loved you. The second time

✦

You loved me, too.
The fifteenth I was sick,
The sixteenth well—
Somewhere, every day, a son gets out of bed.
There are faster ways to get there, simpler ways,

✦

But I like this way best.

IN THE DOLOMITES

1.

The afternoon walk, it turns out, may not have been a walk at all.
Nor can I locate in the Dolomites the place
Where we met, though I remember

It with a level of detail I reserve
For things of consequence.
Snow layered in the crevices, white against black. Impossible

Patches of green where grass
Showed through, and more impossible
The gentians, still blooming, yellow against green.

For the color above our heads, heaven, the sky—
I had no word for that.
No one did; remember

This happened a long time ago.
Even if it existed in the world, in your eyes,
Blue did not exist yet in my mind.

2.

I see a rectangular, steeply sloping meadow.
At the top of the meadow a cottage,
And in front of the cottage door

Two women are standing, one with a kerchief on her head.
Children are gathering flowers,
A girl and a boy, the latter of whom is me.

And because the girl has gathered the more prodigious bunch,
I grab it from her; she runs
Up the meadow in tears. To console her

The woman in a kerchief cuts a slice of black bread,
Then slathers it with with jam.
I throw the flowers to the ground, run to the cottage,

And ask to be given bread, too.
In fact I am given some.
The woman cuts the loaf with a long knife.

3.

When I was young I had a beautiful body.
Don't imagine me proud, you had one, too; everybody did.
Just walking down the street or

Looking out the window, sitting on a train,
Was like staring
Into the sun. Modesty

Made nothing happen
Since the parts
Were more enticing than the whole.

I read a lot of books. I drove
Long distances with the windows down. Who were
The ones with golden eyes and sunlit hair

Who lounged all day beside the river clearly
Doing something important
Though it looked like nothing at all?

4.

At twelve I returned to Bolzano for the first time.
Always I'd longed for the meadows
Of my childhood, where I'd escaped from my father even

When I could barely walk. But when I returned,
Something else excited me greatly:
A thirteen-year-old girl, the daughter of my hosts, who last I'd seen
     at four.

Immediately I fell in love—
My first infatuation,
Though I said nothing to anyone.

After a few days, the girl returned to school, as soon I did, too.
But in the interim I spent my afternoons
Wandering in the meadows, the mountains

Rising, as they always had, abruptly from my feet.
My fantasies were not directed at the future,
But rather sought to improve the past.

5.

Two children walking through the meadow where they were born.
Born there like animals, suckled by a she-wolf
Together in one bed, one bower.

When one of them smiled, they both smiled.
When one of them frowned,
Together they frowned, furrowed their brows, so serious, so stern!

Then together they laughed.
Together they ate, together they slept,
Their legs tangled up together,

Legs brown from the sun.
Together they forgot the past, they invented
The future, the bower, the bed—

Then it was morning. One of us got in the car,
One of us stood at the door
And waved good-bye.

6.

Knowledge, as the ancients remind us,
Is conventional; not in the sense of
Arbitrary, but because it depends

On qualities we cannot observe.
Atom, from *atomos*, meaning indivisible.
So if the atoms of water

Are slippery and smooth,
The atoms of salt are pointed,
While the atoms of red things quiver like flame.

On the color blue Democritus is silent.
So is Homer, who calls the sea
Oinops, wine-dark, or, more literally, wine-looking.

The hides of oxen, to our eyes brown or black,
Also he calls *oinops*. The sky
He calls *starry*, *broad*, *iron*, or *copper*.

7.

I'm looking at a boy and a girl, no longer boy and girl.
Together they have not only the future,
They have a past. She's reading

Letters he's written; he's leaning his head against her neck,
He's curling his arm behind her slender waist,
His fingers emerging, from my viewpoint,

Just below her breast.
Gently they're touching her breast.
Remember how that felt?

Behind them a garden, the meeting, the pursuit.
Is the shrubbery tended or overgrown, the columbines
Luxurious because they're trimmed?

Yellow her bodice, green the trees.
Are the branches closing off the sky, or parting
To reveal it, a smudge of blue?

8.

At this point in the narrative
I remember very little; whole years fall away.
Time, if you'll permit me the expression, stood still.

Yes, there were children of our own, we moved to Treviso.
Then it was morning.
You were standing at the door.

Why won't you come with me,
Why must I go alone,
Asked the first person ever to die.

When finally I admitted, to my shame, *this is the worst thing*
That's ever happened to me,
What had happened was almost nothing.

But I'd never seen it before, I had no
Word to describe it,
Though it was everywhere.

9.

The windows were open, the ledges
Of the balcony broad: the sweep of the canal
And the flutter of the white curtains were an invitation to

—I couldn't have said what. A reef, over which had broken,
Through long ages, the billows of an angry sea?
When the fog rising from the intervening

Plains and lagoons had lifted,
There they were: towers
And ramparts, battlements, pinnacles, the deepest

Of deep reds, the blackest black
Against a cobalt sky.
Mountains, stars, calves, serpents, fever,

War, fame, vice, adultery—these are among the things
That cannot take the place
Of heaven, though people have tried.

10.

In my first life, my body was fresh, unaccustomed to itself.
I learned to read, to make love.
Maybe it was like this for you, too. In my second

I was asked to be older; when I advertised
My interests they proved
Interesting to other people. What interested me?

The trees grew taller, the houses stayed the same.
And when I was summoned again
I had to count out loud—

Was this the fourth time, the fifth?
A stranger remembered me;
You lived here, he said, a long time ago. The trees

Had grown taller, the children were more beautiful than ever
Or had they always been so,
Smiling at one another, staring at the sky?

112TH STREET

If only once, if ever you have the chance,
You should climb a volcano.
The hermitage at base camp, the glasses of brandy—
That's the past.
Who wants to think about the past?

You want to push forward, climb higher, while all around you,
Inches beneath your feet,
Earth is seething, a river of liquid rock.

Will you make it to the summit—
The flying slag, the potholes
Red as an open wound?
Of course you will, it's easy; everybody does.

So little behind you,
So much ahead—

Once, walking up Broadway
Late at night,
Both of us a little drunk, flurries in the air, Christmas trees
Lining the sidewalk, block after block—

At every corner
You kissed me.
Then the light would change.

II

THURSDAY

Because the most difficult part about making something, also the
   best,
Is existing in the middle,
Sustaining an act of radical imagination,
I simmered a broth: onion, lemon, a big handful of mint.

The phone rang. So with my left
Hand I answered it,
Sautéing the rice, then adding the broth
Slowly, one ladle at a time, with my right—*hello?*—

The miracle, it's easy to miss, is the moment when the husks
   dissolve,
Each grain releasing its tiny explosion of starch.

If you take it off the heat just then, let it sit
While you shave the parmesan into paper-thin curls,
It will be perfectly creamy,
But will still have a bite.

There will be dishes to do,
The moon will rise,
And everyone you love will be safe.

SINCE FEBRUARY

Russ

Your mother is driving you out of Texas,
She's heading east on Route 10,
The top is down, the wind is blowing through her hair.

Chattanooga? That was hours ago.
Martinsburg, Harrisburg—
You've never seen the ocean, you could see the ocean—

First stop: the Vermeers
At the Metropolitan, gallery 899.
Second, Maria Callas, seats in the parterre.

Mark

Eyebrows raised as you uncorked the cognac, dishes cleared,
The children screaming in the living room—
Grow old along with me.

Eight years later resting on a bench
In the Piazza Santo Spirito—
Getting old is not for sissies.

You by the window overlooking the park at Ninety-First Street,
Unable to walk
There, looking to read.

Wendy

Addio, per sempre addio, per sempre,
Sings Elisabetta to Don Carlo at the end of act five;
Per sempre, sings the don. Inevitably

This story ends, we had a train to make.
Feet dangling beneath you,
One of us hoisting you by your left arm, another by your right,

You flew down the Via Venti Settembre
While the rest of us ran.
Your beaming face.

Bianca

Although we're standing on the icy wing of an airplane
In the middle of the Hudson River,
Nobody dies today.

Although the ruins of Palmyra have been ruined again,
Ruins I saw first in *Life* magazine,
I was a boy, summer of '66,

Nobody dies today. All we did
Was leave the door open.
And you disappeared.

Sandy

After the torchlight red on sweaty faces,
The lectures and the arguments,
The students listening politely in rows—

You with a bottle of chardonnay and a package of Ritz crackers
Pinched from the reception.
Meet you in my room!

And a thousand years before that: you
At the Academy, letting me sit
In Edith Wharton's chair.

Maureen

I'm wearing the cardigan you sent me, the blue one;
I saved the box in which it came.
I'm walking across the park, I'm sitting

In brilliant sunshine on the steps of the museum, a taxi pulls up—
Everybody's alive.
Where is he exactly,

You asked, unable to imagine
A life alone.
Where are you now?

Russ

A singer in the moment before he opens his mouth,
Said Charles Anthony, who stood on the Met stage 2,928 times,
Is the loneliest person in the world.

Love of words, mouths shaping words, your taste, equally exquisite,
For the vulgar—I dreamt
About a department meeting: there, primly

At a little desk, you were waiting.
What are you doing here?
Where else, you answered, *would I be?*

IN THE VILLAGE

1.

Shortly before I died,
Or possibly after,
I moved to a small village by the sea.

You'll recognize it, as did I, because I've written
About this village before.
The rocky sliver of land, the little houses where the fishermen once
    lived—

We had everything we needed: a couple of rooms
Overlooking the harbor,
A small collection of books,
Paperbacks, the pages
Brittle with age.

How, if I'd never seen
The village, had I pictured it so accurately?
How did I know we'd be happy there,
Happier than ever before?

The books reminded me of what,
In our youth,
We called literature.

2.

The sentences I've just written
Took it out of me.
I searched for the words,
And I resisted them as soon as I put them down.

Now, listening to them again, what I hear
Is not so much nostalgia
As a love of beginning. A wish

Not to be removed
From time but
Always to be immersed in it.
The boats come in, the boats go out—

3.

After a routine ultrasound revealed a fifteen-centimeter mass, my left kidney was removed robotically on February 12. Fifteen months later, nodules were discovered in my lungs and peritoneum. Two subsequent rounds of therapy failed to impede their growth, so I enrolled in a trial, a treatment not yet FDA approved.

I walked down High Street to the harbor, though when I say *walked* I mean imagined; I hadn't been there yet.

4.

Of ghosts pursued, forgotten, sought anew—
Everywhere I go
The trees are full of them.

From trees come books, that, when they open,
Lead you to expect a person
On the other side:

One hand having pulled
The doorknob
Toward him, the other

Held out, open,
Beckoning
You forward—

5.

The Branch Will Not Break.

A Cold Spring.

Leaflets.

The Lost World.

The Moving Target.

Nightmare Begins Responsibility.

Rivers and Mountains.

The Story of Our Lives.

Untitled Subjects.

Water Street.

6.

Ash-blond, tall, a sweater
Knotted by its sleeves around his neck,
A boy is leaning on a bicycle. Deftly when she reaches him

A girl slips to the grass, one hand straightening her skirt,
The other tugging at the boy,
Who remains standing, to sit beside her.

Their heads are close
Enough to be touching;
Their lips are still—

A book is the future.
You dream
Of reading it, and once you've finished, it's a miracle, you know the
    past.

The sky fills with stars. The sun
Climbs every morning
Over Watch Hill, dropping behind the harbor at dusk.

Water Street runs past
Church and Wall,
Harmony and School,
Until it crosses Omega, by the sea.

VENICE

Before the pedestrian bridges had railings, before most people knew how to swim, the water entrance would have been the Hotel Daniele's fulcrum, the hub of its staff's solicitations. *The beginning of everything was in seeing the gondola-beak come actually inside the door at the Daniele*: for centuries it's been impossible to see Venice except through the images of Canaletto and Turner, the sentences of Shakespeare and Byron, but the teen-aged John Ruskin nonetheless experienced the beginning of everything—not just a discovery of a lifelong passion for Venice but the discovery of eros itself.

✦

Nobody has been there before. Every time you walk from a typically mid-century train station onto the water—the vaporetti unloading their cargo of tourists, the dome of San Simeone Piccolo hovering on the other side, improbably larger than the portico beneath it—you do so for the first time. Even when you know the city well enough to navigate alone, getting lost is easy, but so is being found—look where I am! Walk out to the Ognissanti at nine o'clock at night, the water black and still, look down toward San Nicolò dei Mendicoli, founded in the seventh century, built over the next millennium, and you might be anyone living in the year 2020 or 1520.

✦

I grew up in New Jersey, not far from New York, not far from the Jersey shore. Though New Jersey has more coastline per square mile than Alaska or Hawaii, water seemed to me exotic. Cranford, the town next door, where my father taught art at the high school, is bisected by the meandering Rahway River, and after Hurricane Alma in the summer of '66, the river's twists and turns were obliterated, the houses along its banks submerged in a vast sheet of shimmering water.

✦

Venice, as everyone knows, is sinking. Its buildings settle a little deeper, year after year, into the layer of silt on which they were made. At the same time, the water is rising, transgressing the layers of impervious Istrian stone laid on a foundation of innumerable tree trunks. The lagoon is the crux of Venetian hegemony: in what other medieval city does the center of government, the home of its ruler, stand completely unprotected, meters from the sea, flaunting its delicate opulence? But as the level of the lagoon rises, salt water wicks into the courses of brick laid above the stone. The MOSE project, an expensive plan to install mobile barriers at the mouths of the lagoon, has been debated for decades, and meanwhile the atrium of San Marco floods over half the days of the year.

✦

Like anyone, I could slip in the bathtub. Looking at myself in the mirror, I was forced to rethink everything: returning to Venice bolstered my relationship to contingency, though I can't evade the suspicion that New Jersey might have suited me just as well.

✦

Start in the northwest corner of the Campo San Giacomo, behind the garden with its stand of sycamores. Take a right on the first bridge crossing the canal, turn sharply to the left, as quickly you must, then take another right on the Calle del Tentor. If you keep walking straight, or as straight as you can, you'll come to the Campo Santa Maria Mater Domini, unremarkable except for the row of elegant Gothic windows gracing the dilapidated fourteenth-century Palazzetto Viaro on its west side. Beneath the central window is a low relief of the Venetian lion, symbol of the Republic, that was half scratched out by Napoleon's soldiers in 1797, when after a thousand years of independence the Republic welcomed an outsider.

VIA SACRA

Imagine the most beautiful girl in the world is walking in front of
    you.
She's entering the ruins of western civilization,
The wind is swirling her skirt
Around her thighs.

You want to follow. But you know
She wants to be alone
With western civilization; she's holding a map.

Little boy, one day your hand will hover above the spinning record
As you drop
The stylus on the Berg quartet.

You will retain this memory, return to it,
Because she'll write it down.

III

BARCAROLLE

Empedocles on Etna is a poem
By the Victorian poet Matthew Arnold.
Readily I'll concede that poetry is a criticism of life (his phrase)
About as much as red-hot iron
Is a criticism of fire,

✦

But we're in Sicily.
The gods are still with us.
The sun has warmed the rocks
On which we're lounging, eating goat cheese, drinking new wine.
You're hardly wearing any clothes.

✦

Nobody's wearing clothes!
Neither is anyone
Worried about sunlight.
This is before Jesus, before Socrates,
Before the double onslaught of guilt and rationality

✦

Doomed us (I'm paraphrasing Nietzsche) to believe
In the rectification of the world
Through knowledge—to live
Within the limited circle of soluble problems,
Where we may cheerfully say to life

I want you! You're worth knowing!
Empedocles is having a bad day.
Once, he was a god;
Smart, good-looking, too.
You understand how anyone might feel that way

Just being where we are, tasting things, just breathing the air.
Above us, Etna's cone
Emits its languorous white plume.
Miracles? *Mistrust them,* says Empedocles.
Mind is a spell that governs

Heaven and earth.
Is it so small a thing
To have enjoyed the sun,
To have lived lightly in the spring,
To have loved, to have thought, to have done?

Obvious as the answer to this question may be, convincing, too,
Empedocles climbs beyond the ashen trees,
The potholes red as an open wound,
And steps into a cloud.
A poem of passive suffering, said Arnold,

＋

Could have no place in his collected poems.
No place. His greatest poem! Whose suffering
Isn't passive? What else
Could suffering be?
One night in Venice

＋

I couldn't sleep; I heard the bells
Of San Giacomo ring four times, then five.
I heard the mutter of a boat, two voices, a woman's and a man's,
Then somehow rising
Between them, as from the water itself,

＋

The Chopin *Barcarolle.*
Who could they have been?
Why were they playing
Chopin in their little boat,
Playing it softly, just for me? Remember

＋

When we lived like forest creatures,
You and I, when all
We left behind were footsteps
Crushed in the wet grass?
When I opened my eyes

✦

Sun-stirred water played
Across the ceiling;
You were asleep.
It felt like being
In the present, being alive.

SCHOOL STREET

The person I once was found himself
In the present, which was the only place he could be.
The dog that yesterday had barked
At his empty dish barked again.
The stars were still shining,
Though the brilliance of the sun obscured them so completely
You'd believe they'd disappeared.
Time to walk to the paddock.
Will the roses be blooming? Will Penny be there, too?
Selfishly we planted cornflowers, delphiniums,
A different bed for every shade.
From behind the wisteria came children, then grandchildren—
The girls wore smocked dresses, dresses my mother
Had made, the boys had floppy hair.
The things we made
Ourselves seemed permanent,
But like the stars invisible, even the things
We made from words. Downstairs
The kitchen, the living room, everything in place:
The bed could fold up in the wall.
But upstairs a ladder where each evening, one by one,
We'd climb into the crow's nest
To rehearse the stars. Hold the railing! Don't fall!
How did we afford this house?
Why, if it exists
In the present,
Am I speaking in the past?

SONG OF THE SUN

1.

Two children side by side
In the cathedral at twilight, knowing
They'd missed the train.
And once, just
Before dawn, they stumbled
Down an alley, it was Christmas,
To a courtyard strung with tiny yellow lights.
They learned to read,
To make love. The fields
Grew taller than their foreheads,
And the trees sent taproots
Deep into the ground.

2.

What happened next
Had never happened before
Though it would happen again.
From her body came forth another body not
More beautiful but beautiful
In a different way.
Immediately
There were people who helped them care for this body,
Feed it, clothe it,
But when this happened
Again, it had never
Happened before.

3.
Song of the First First Child

In the middle of a steep staircase
I fell asleep I didn't know
Whether to look forward
Or back each step
Looked dangerous to me
You called this being born I call it
Making a sandwich
Taking the bus if
You could understand me
I would tell you
Everything I'd show you
Sunlight on my golden hair

4.
Song of the Second First Child

Before I could walk I
Walked through snow a forest
Shagged with ice who's there
Said the bird I could not
Say I could say
Only what I'd heard before I said
It differently there was
A little girl she could not
Speak she spoke
The pine trees
Shagged with ice she said
You're beautiful

5.

To imagine you've changed is to preserve
The person you once were.
Alternatively, to recognize you've
Never changed, that now you
See yourself as then you
Didn't, couldn't,
Even if you'd tried,
Is to feel
Viscerally a part
Of time, to collaborate
In the project of becoming, always
To have begun.

6.

What happens next takes
Seconds, it takes a thousand years.
A dog barks once,
A cricket chirps, the children
Lift their heads to breathe in fields, a flag
Snapping in the wind, the sun
A daub of Tintoretto's
Crimson sliding into the Great Salt Pond—let's
Count together,
Kathryn, Alice, Marc,
Jillian, Owen, Adam, everybody,
Five, four, three, two—

7.
Song of the Sun

No matter where
You are no
Matter where I
Go if you are
Speaking
To me I have
Said this
Before I say
It now I will be
Listening
To you
Speak

THIS LITTLE ISLAND

1.

Outside the room where you have lived a long time
Are other rooms, another building, just like yours.

Each night a ship sails past, wider than the building, taller than the
    highest church.
And though the passengers come to visit the city,
No one in the city ever boards the ship. Would you?

Each night this spectacle is seen by you.
The street surveyed,
The air inhaled.

Grapes from the west,
Cinnamon from the east—

If I've employed too liberally the passive voice,
Remember it's the thoughts, the feelings
That matter here,
Not the one who feels them.

2.

Shall we walk to the market?
You could walk there blind, like Gloucester, smelling your way.

Shall we stop for coffee? Which café?
The one that's commandeered by women, delicate cups?
Or the one where men preside, baristas in tuxedos, the coffee rich
    enough for rainy days?

A window, the desk, a lamp and a chair—
You've liked the room, you like to rearrange it for winter,
Put things back for spring.

But you've been young for a long time,
An embarrassingly long time.
Look what you wrote!
Remember how much, despite
Your ridiculous behavior, you've been loved.

3.

The city never changes, it's never the same.
Sometimes the inhabitants restore a building, patch it up,
But in a generation they're dissatisfied, they try again,
Expose the old parts so you see them
Plainly, ruined or not.

Who schooled you?
What made you scared of change?

Vividly you remember a child's body; likewise you remember a
    man's.
You woke up one morning,
There you were, a stinking adult.

What happened between? What will it be like,
You've seen the images, to watch your body spoiling
From the inside out, your lungs, your neck,
The muscles in your face—

Look out the window,
Choose a single brick.
Once, a long time ago, the city was old.

4.

Clouds desire the sky, the sky the sun. The wave
Desires the land it's eroding,
Repeating the same question, day after day—
Am I allowed to ask for what I want?

And every day the land responds
Of course you're allowed.
You're allowed to be angry,
You're allowed to curse the God who put you here.

I've buried many people, old people, young people.
I've buried children while their parents wept beside the grave.

But I've also seen miracles.
Remember when they told you
You might die? You didn't, you're alive.
And every month since then, every second is a miracle.

What happens next you cannot know.
Is it better or worse to live a long time?
Really the words better and worse do not obtain.

And when the land stops speaking
The wave flows out to sea.

5.

Close your eyes, unclench your hands.
Relax each muscle in your body, first your forehead, then your neck,
Your chest, your arms, how young you are, you've never
Done this before, you've done it a thousand times—

Outside, the walls of San Trovaso are streaked with gold.
Boats are knocking against the Giudecca.
If you stand on tiptoes you can see, above the chimney pots, its
     glistening rim.

Look at all the people, look at their dogs! They're nothing like you,
And they're here.
Who brought you here, who made the bed?

That gasp of pleasure when you entered the room,
First touched the walls,
Whose was it, if it wasn't yours?

FOREVER

Once, in a room no bigger than the bed,
I made love with a girl.

✦

Have you ever made love with a girl?
Once I hadn't, then I had.

✦

A girl was looking up at me,
She was lying on the grass.

✦

Once, after a terrible fight, I made love with a girl.
We were children again.

✦

Once, eating ice cream,
I smelled her body on my hands.

✦

The first time I made love with a girl I was scared; I thought I
would hurt her.

✦

Once in Italy and on the same day,
Once in France.

✦

Remember that week in the cabin?
The time in front of the fire, when everyone else was asleep?

✦

Once, we made love to make a baby.
Once, a baby was sleeping on the bed.

✦

I walked across the park.
A girl pulled her jeans off slowly.

✦

Once, making love with a girl,
I thought I was someone else.

✦

I was a boy forever.
She pushed me down on the bed.

✦

What did we do afterward?
What had I done before?

✦

Once, without my noticing, the world turned once,
Then twice, then disappeared.

✦

Turned twice, and everything
Was different, everything was the same.

✦

Nobody lives forever.
I love you. I love you, too.

✦

Once, in a world no bigger than a bed,
You said we'd be lovers forever.

✦

That was the first time.
The second was by the sea.

Earthling
(2017)

Earthling, noun.
Forms: irþling, yrþling, ærðling, eorðling.

1. A ploughman, a cultivator of the soil.

2. A kind of bird (not identified).

I

SUITCASE

No one can predict the size, the shape, or even the location
Of the room where you will live a long time,
But every time you pack
You're thinking about that room.

You're imagining the color of the draperies,
You're deciding the desk should face the window in summer,
When the sun is overhead,
But face the wall in winter,
When the light's so low it hits you in the eyes.

In winter there are no distractions, you study the wall.
But in summer the trolley stops in front of the Ministry of
    Public Instruction.

Usually it sits there, nobody moves, but sometimes
It's crossing the river.
Little houses, new apartments,
Bodies smelling fresh in the morning, rank at night—

When I pack, I lay out every sock, each pair
Of shorts without a fold.
If my shirts are too large to lie down flat,
I tuck their arms beneath their sides to fill the suitcase perfectly.
A window, the desk, a lamp and a chair.

One of life's greatest pleasures,
If I'm allowed the phrase,
Is packing a suitcase.

It's not like building a fire,
When you want to leave space for air.

COMPLAINT

Walk out the front door, the dog tugs
Boyishly at the leash.
I sit at my desk. A breeze
Floats up from Oakdale on the hottest day of the year.
This is the climate of reason.

But in the climate of no reason
I look out the window at midnight.
My mother appears in a red coat, raking the leaves.

Always she wore that coat in autumn,
The tattered wool, the large
Black buttons, but only to rake leaves.

Walk out the front door, somebody dies.
Walk out the back,
The rabbit jumps out of its hole.
Kitchen in one world, bedroom in another—

You could say it's always
September here,
Too warm, then cold,
Every day the first day of school.

The bus is waiting.
I've got books, my lunch,
My gym clothes in a plastic bag.

THE CROCODILE

1.

What I wanted was to lift my body in unnatural postures
High above the earth, to dance,
To live beyond ideas.
Imagine feeling assured you were beautiful.
Girls wanted to run their fingers on my skin, also guys; I bit off
  their hands.

If called to, I could wait beneath the water a long time.
I could let a bird pick leeches from my tongue.

So in the moment of youth when other people embrace passion
I fell back on discipline. My throat
Was capable of many different sounds but the pleasure
Was in keeping silent, letting parts of me be seen.
Sometimes a plover mistook me for a log
But that's not deception; I really look like a log.

I survived the great extinctions,
I pretended to be myself.
To let you know me, I need only move my eyes.

2.

Like me, you had a father and a mother,
You grew up in a particular place, a particular time.
Your skin displays the scars of that place.

You've decapitated chickens, eviscerated live fish.
You carry yourself with what, to other people, seems aplomb,
But the impulse driving such behaviors,
Necessary in themselves, has infiltrated daily life. In arguments
You'll drag another person underwater till he drowns.

Though I grew very large, though I developed great capacity of mind,
I was afraid of my mother. Afraid not just of scrutiny
But of being the object of someone's pride.
What was I protecting?
She was willful, yes,
But tiny, generous to a fault.

In Egypt, the family crocodiles were adorned
With bracelets, earrings of molten gold.
Then mummified, laid out in the tombs.
The word itself is from the Greek:
Krokodeilus, pebble worm.

3.

What manner of thing is your crocodile?

✦

It is shaped, sir, like itself, and it is as broad as it has breadth;
it is just so high as it is, and moves with its own organs. It lives
by that which nourishes it, and the elements once out of it, it
transmigrates.

✦

What color is it of?

✦

Of its own color, too.

✦

'Tis a strange serpent.

✦

'Tis so, and the tears of it are wet.

—*Antony and Cleopatra, II.7*

4.

As a child, I was given a stuffed crocodile.
Don't think this strange; most humans have dolls resembling
 themselves.
My sister had one, too.

Tiny marbles filled the sockets of its eyes.
The skin was stitched together up the belly, where it's soft,
And though it was only a foot, perhaps ten inches long,
The jaws were clamped together with a tack.

Presumably this kept the little row of teeth from hurting you,
But the tack protruded from the bottom of its chin,
Sharper than any tooth.
I remember rubbing over it, back and forth.

When my mother died,
I was right beside her.
She'd been unconscious for a day.
My sister and my father were there, too.

I leaned down close to her left ear, I whispered,
Thank you for everything you did for me,
Thank you especially for what you did for our girls.

Then, immediately, the color left her face,
She was no longer in her body,
And she sank beneath the lagoon.

5.

Picture, by way of analogy, a mountain range.
Some interruption of traffic, perhaps a flood, has blocked the roads,
But communication between the villages is maintained over steep
    footpaths,
The kind used ordinarily by hunters, originally by their prey.

Some people speak more openly by inefficient means.
And the steeper the path, the more
Arduous the climb,
The more likely we are to believe.

Someday I won't be hungry.
I'll watch an egret stepping through the reeds.

The miser imagines there's a certain sum to fill his heart
But for sorrow there's no remedy.
It requires what it cannot hope.
We've known each other, earth, a long time.

When the light rests low on the Nile, the Ganges, the Everglades—
I could be anywhere—
Day is discontinued, motionless.
A voice is what you have.

THE DISHWASHER

For many years I saved my money, bought a car, a used Chevette.
Lean on me, said the radio, *when you're not strong.*

I'd known that song since I was young but every time I heard it
I wanted to hear it again.
I drove to the supermarket, then drove home.
I looked in the refrigerator, under the bed.

As if I were standing in the kitchen, unloading the dishwasher,
    holding the phone,
I heard my mother's voice.
I heard it plainly, as if she were standing in the room.

I know it's early, she said,
But I'm planning ahead for Christmas.

So I'd like to remember: What kind of coffee do you like?
Regular, or decaf, or both at certain times?
I want to be prepared, in case you'd like a cup when you're here.

BOOK THREE

Long ago, before you were born,
I lived in a house at the edge of a forest.
It was a yellow house; you've heard me speak of it before.
Much of what happened in the house was interesting, even
  amusing,
But at times I felt weighed down by a sadness

✦

Impossible to overcome,
As if I lived at the bottom of a dark pit,
No prospect but a slender aspen tree against the sky.
Languidly, but not idly, one morning I began to draw the tree.
Its lines insisted upon being followed,

✦

And as one branch rose from another, finding its place
In the air, the tree became more beautiful.
By laws finer than any known to me
The tree composed itself,
And when at last it was there in front of me, looking back,

✦

Everything I'd ever thought about trees had disappeared.
As for the pit, the furies, the snakes,
The gloomy caverns and the burning lakes,

And last, and most, if these were cast behind,
The avenging horror of a conscious mind—

✦

They neither are, nor were, nor ever can be
(Lucretius, *On the Nature of Things*, Book III).
All my life I prayed I'd die quickly.
But if death were but the absence of consciousness,
Like a long sleep unbroken by dreams,

✦

I wouldn't be able to see you; neither
Could you hear me speak.
You're looking out the window, your feet on a chair.
Anyone who didn't know you would presume
You're waiting for something to happen

✦

But in fact it's happening now.

II

BY THE SAME AUTHOR

Today, no matter if it rains,
It's time to follow the path into the forest.

The same people will be walking the same dogs,
Or if not the same dogs, dogs that behave in similar fashions,
Some barking, some standing aloof.
The owners carry plastic bags.

But this is the forest, they complain, we must do as we like.
We must let the dogs run free,
We must follow their example,
The way we did when we were young.

Back then we slept, watched TV—
We were the dogs.
By the time the screen door slammed, we were gone.

Nobody really talks like that in the forest.
They're proud of their dogs,
Proud especially of the ones who never bark.
They're upset about the Norway maple, it's everywhere,
Crowding out the hickories and oaks.

Did you know it takes a million seeds to make one tree?
Your chances of surviving in the forest,
Of replicating yourself, are slim.

Today, the smaller dogs are wearing raincoats,
The bigger ones are stiffing it out.
They're tense, preoccupied,
Running in circles,
Getting tangled in the leash.

It's hard remaining human in the forest.
To move the limbs of the body,
To speak intelligible words,
These things promise change.

SILVER SWAN

The streets were old, but all the people were young,
Striding forward with great purpose,
Girls smiling openly in the faces of boys.

Not every boy noticed, but we all kept walking forward,
Over the bridges, under the trees,
Streets not growing wider
But the buildings growing taller, taller than the trees,
And not just taller but more mannered, ornamental, asking also
    to be seen.

How did this happen? Where were our parents, our teachers,
People who long before us had worn
Footpaths into roads, roads into thoroughfares?

We walked to the park, to the station,
Skin beneath our sideburns soft as a girl's.
We watched the swan's nest growing larger
Though we never saw the swan build anything.

It sat along the riverbank or floated placidly across the water
Like a Schubert song, the tenor unaware
Of the piano beneath, the left hand
Indistinguishable from the right—

In time, we observed in one another a sadness,
Not bitter, a resignation
That made our actions, no matter
How many times we repeated them, feel complete.

ARCADIA

1.

Just as there were reeds along the riverbank,
Just as there were clouds
Above my head, my lute was lying beside me on the grass.

I placed the little finger of my right hand on the soundboard,
Just below the strings.
Not the tip of the finger, the side.

I curled the palm of my right hand toward me,
Covering the strings, so that I played
The bass note with the thumb,
The next with the index,
And the top note with the third.

The sun retreated, the night turned cold.
Rain began to fall, softly at first,
Though surely rain had fallen here before, as rain falls
    everywhere.

With my left hand, I positioned my thumb and index finger
Opposite each other, bearing no weight,
As if the neck of the lute were not there.

2.

At this they all laughed.

Then the Count began afresh: My lords, he said, I am not pleased if the young man is not also a musician, and if, besides his cunning upon the book, he have not skill in like manner on sundry instruments. There is no ease of labor more honest and more praise-worthy, especially at court, where many things are taken in hand to please women, whose tender breasts are soon pierced with melody.

Then the Lord Gasper: I believe music, he said, together with other vanities, is mete for women, also for them that have the likeness of men, but not for them that be men indeed, who ought not with such delicacies womanize their minds and so bring themselves to dread death.

—The First Booke of the Courtyer of
Count Baldessar Castilio

3.

For many years I lived apart, in happy oblivion.
In retrospect, I understand I'd been a child,
Though lacking comparisons I couldn't have said so.

I learned things, things no child, left to himself, could possibly know.
My head, which had been empty, now was full.

My head would grow larger.
How could it not?

At night, standing in the shower, I closed my eyes.
The water trickled down my forehead
To my nose, from my nose to my lips, my chin, then disappeared.

But some of what stayed in my head
Should not have been there.

4.

Listen, said the reeds along the riverbank: the nymphs
Are weeping for Daphnis.
His mother embraces his body, railing against the stars.

Nobody drives his cattle to the cool stream, no one could drink;
The mountains echo with the beasts of the desert.

Daphnis, it was you who yoked them to the chariot,
Who led us in the dance, weaving
Together vine leaves with reeds.

The vine exceeds the tree on which it climbs.
The grape exceeds the vine,
The calf the herd, the corn the field.

Now, where we planted barley, thistles grow.
Where once were violets, hyacinths—nothing but weeds.

Scatter the ground with flowers, shepherds,
Set out two bowls,
One of milk and one of oil.
Then carve these verses on his tomb.

5.

When I painted, everybody saw.
When I played, everybody heard.

I ate your raspberries.
The sign *No Trespassing* applied to me.

Now, the hemlocks have grown higher than the house.
There's moss on my stoop, a little mildew
In the shower but you've never seen my shower.

I can undress by the window,
I can sleep in the barn.

The sky, which is cloudy,
Suits the earth to which it belongs.

EARTHLING

Above our heads they're making pies.
They're cutting butter
Into tiny pieces, they're discussing its advantages over lard.

Together we will sit around the table
And the servings will be generous, first the apple, then the
    pumpkin—

Do we have to eat now?

I can smell the nutmeg.
I can hear the flour sifting to the bowl.

PETITE MAISON

In the village was a bar, a bistro, you might say,
Though really it was someone's home.
In the kitchen I could see a stove
No larger than our own,
And by the time we ordered

✦

There was no more chicken, only lamb;
The locals ate there every night.
The next morning we walked to the market.
We filled our satchels not only
With fruits and vegetables

✦

But with oils, spices, a set of wooden spoons.
We scrubbed our refrigerator,
We bought more food than it could hold.
But at the end of the day it was not fatigue
That returned us to the bar,

✦

It was habit, as if we'd lived in the village all our lives.
Probably we lingered over the wine,
Surely we walked home,
The leaves would have been turning, it was September,
The moon a little dollop of red fire—

＊

I realize that all my life I rarely
Spoke this way; nihilism
Was my defense against the glamour of fortitude.
But in the paths of creation, in the darkness and the light,
Things seem bad when really

＊

They're at variance with other things.
With things we may not see
They're in accord.
Then they are good; in themselves, too, they are good.
The next morning, when we awoke

＊

To find the bar was gone, the shutters closed,
The few chairs scattered at the curb,
I asked the earth if we should stay here, make this our home.
Earth said you must never leave,
You must stay here forever.

ALLEGORY

1.

In the Forest of Wearisome Sadness,
Where often I've found myself wandering alone,
I met my heart, who called to me, asking me where I was going.

The path was long and straight, row after row of conifers
    receding
To a horizon that because of the geometry
Seemed farther than it really was,
Like the door at the top of a staircase in Versailles.

But as if the forest's maker had been offended by elegance,
A pile of rocks disrupted the rows: the forest once
Had been a field. I remember that field.

I was carried there by my father, beside him
My grandfather, who planted the trees.
Until they were tall enough to survive,
He mowed the field, piling up rocks, taking down brush with a
    scythe.

How, since I've known the forest almost since birth, could I have
    been lost?
Why, since the forest is beautiful, is it not a place of delight?

Repeatedly I asked these questions of my heart,
But like a good physician, he elected
To keep silent, leaving me to answer for myself.

2.

Late at night, when I'm lying in bed and cannot sleep,
My heart reads to me from the Romance of Pleasant Thought.
Always I've heard the story before, and typically,
Since the stories are true, I am their hero.

I'm riding my tricycle on the sidewalk near the house where I was
    born.
Because I am unsupervised, I indulge in what seems at the
    moment
A daring wish: I ride the tricycle beneath a sprinkler.

Immediately I am overcome with remorse.
Evidence of my trespass is everywhere to be seen,
And for the first time in my life I contemplate a lie.

Would my shirt dry faster if I stood in the sun, where it's hot,
Or in the shade, where cool breezes rustle the leaves?

In the version of this story that appears now
In the Romance of Pleasant Thought,
I admire not so much my ingenuity
As the evidence of my early devotion to empiricism,
The way I manage terror by examining how things work.

3.

It's done, there's nothing more to say.
My heart is gone from me.
Because he has fallen in love
He has abandoned me.

It's pointless making myself uncomfortable over this
By being mournful or sad.
It's done, there's nothing more to say.
My heart is gone from me.

He does nothing but mock me.
When I tell him pitifully
That I cannot live on my own,
He does not listen.
It's done, there's nothing more to say.

—after Charles d'Orléans

4.

Imagine you've been in love forever, since before you were born.
You walk the field. At every third step
You scoop out a handful of wheat
From the seed bag, scattering it broadcast.
As the sun comes up you're walking in a golden cloud.

Inside the cloud, time no longer exists.
Your back's not bent, your body is a boy's.

Outside, since it's time for wheat,
The summer rains are finished.
Otherwise it's oats. Every third year it's clover.

The advantage to people like you,
Though there are many disadvantages, is this:
When the earth no longer needs what you can grow,
You plant hundreds, then thousands
Of seedlings, conifers, trees that bear no edible fruit.

Do not imagine yourself sad; you are a servant,
Guided by a fate much more substantial than your own.

You arrange the trees in rows, you tend them,
You're proud of them.
You watch the forest reappear.

III

LYRIC KNOWLEDGE

Finally having cleaned out the closet, I awoke
To find it filled with things.
Somebody else might need those things,
So I put them in a box, I put the box at the curb.

The following morning, after breakfast, the closet once again
  was full.
Once again I cleaned it, this time retaining things
Unfamiliar to me, discarding the rest.

In my mind, these acts of accumulation transpired
As quickly as the acts of dispersal,
A single night, a single day.
In fact they took many years.

In one of those years I wrote a book.
Rather than discarding things
Outright, I redeployed them, altering their function.

But at the end of the year I nonetheless found myself at the curb.
I greeted my neighbors, I was greeted in turn.

Together we watched the cars go by.
The cars followed the road. Above our heads
The leaves turned silver in the breeze.

PREFACE TO AN UNWRITTEN BOOK

Probably you never noticed the portrait
Hanging beside the stairs:
A young woman, though now she'd be about my age.
I had it painted when she died.
Somehow in the fifty years since then

✦

This house has grown up around her,
The few books written,
The many I've read.
But in summer, in early evening,
There's really nothing I'd rather do

✦

Than sit here on the stairs.
We work in the dark,
As Henry James once said,
We do what we can, we give what we have.
As for the book I'm supposed to be writing now—

✦

If you think I should do it, Jim, I will.
But you should realize I'd much rather spend my time
Reading or, since it's the end
Of summer, sitting.
Our truest impulses are so immature

That most of us can't recognize them,
Much less have the fortitude
To carry them out.
I've needed to remain
Mysterious, even to me.

CLIMATE OF REASON

1.

Whenever I find myself growing grim about the mouth,
Whenever it is a drizzly November in my soul,
I get myself to the desert,
Where there is only rock and sand.

Just thinking about it, making sentences
About it, some of the words
Borrowed, some of them my own, is almost enough.
I bring a water bottle and a book.

At this point, the same thing always happens: I pour the water on
    the ground.
As quickly as it leaves the bottle,
Glistening for a moment in sunlight, the water evaporates.

Sometimes I spend the night there, curled up on the sand.
I imagine the beasts of the desert
Circling me, lions and wolves protecting me.

But most nights I return to the house from which I came.
I sleep in a bed where recently another man died.
A headboard, two pillows, a quilt
That someone long ago stitched by hand.
My mother stitched quilts by hand.

When I return to the desert the next morning,
A tree has grown up where I poured the water.
All day I sit beneath the branches.

2.

Enfeebled by prolonged fasting,
The hermit is unable to concentrate on holy things.

His thoughts wander. Memories of his past
Evoke regrets he can no longer suppress,
And as memory begets memory,
He turns ever more deeply into himself.

He rehearses his flight from home, his mother, her perfume.
He remembers his visit to Alexandria,
The slender bodies of both girls and boys.

Involuntarily he yields to the dissatisfaction growing inside him.
Grace departs from him; hope burns low in his heart.

He dreams of the Maccabees slaughtering their enemies
And desires that he might do likewise
With the Alexandrians.
He indulges in reveries concerning the riches of biblical kings.

The Sphinx, the Chimera, all the abnormalities
Described by Herodotus he beholds.
Grotesqueries made animate,
A Sabbath of abominations—

As if everything inside him had spoiled.

Sand-drifts follow the course of the winds,
Rising and falling like great shrouds.

3.

I could go on like this; there's nothing in the desert but time.
Time to read, to think, but mostly
Time to read nothing, to think about nothing.

You go there encumbered, needing to be alone,
And in almost no time you're lonely, which is what you want,
But also what you dread, the landscape stretching far as you can see.

Nothing but rubble. Mountains
In the distance red against a cobalt sky.

One minute you're sharing a good bottle of wine,
You're eating tortelloni stuffed with ricotta and pear,
A little sautéed kale on the side.

Then you're in the desert,
There's work to do.

The desert says
Study that tree,
What is it like?

A silly old man.

4.

A certain man, revered by the Fathers,
Was living in the desert of Porphyrio.
For sustenance he had a date palm over his head, a small garden
    at his feet.
When the date palm sprouted new branches,
He collected the dead ones, thinking they might someday be of use.

Have you ever lived alone a long time?
Then you know that for the hours when the sun appears
Unmoving, directly overhead,
This man was beset with fatigue, as if recovering from a long
    journey.

He turned his head anxiously, first to the left, then to the right,
To see if anyone approached.
He called to the beasts
Of the desert, that they might return.

No one to talk to. Nothing to see.
So while it was a journey of seven days to the nearest city,
Making the conveyance of his handiwork more costly
Than the sum such handiwork might fetch,
He began to weave baskets,
Slowly at first, then with great dexterity.

The brighter the sunlight,
The more intricate his designs.

The date palm dropped more branches,
The days passed quickly as the nights.
And at the end of the year, when his hut was filled to capacity,
He burned the baskets,
Mixing the ashes into the soil.

5.
Song of the Desert

Once I was a girl, I fell in love. Against my better judgment
I allowed myself to fall in love.

Then I was not

A girl, I was the earth.
Pour me a glass of water, once I was the sea.

6.
Song of the Basket

Had you permitted it, earth,
I would have loved
You like a little bird
That picks up crumbs.

7.

Essentially, an artist's work consists of giving life
To the dead matter of the material world.
That matter is the artist's medium.

The artist is in love with it.
He may, as lovers do,
Selfishly expect that what he loves loves him.

But if the artist loves the medium enough to submit to its
    real qualities,
Refusing to exaggerate how they might please him,
The result may justify his idealization.

Such artists fear not so much boredom
As work without pleasure.
In fact, if their work is to succeed,
They require boredom.
They must wait for its effect.

Moments when the artist in each of us created
The material world by finding the unfamiliar in the familiar,
By finding what we'd never known to be ourselves
In what seemed dead—
Such moments are forgotten by most people.

Or else they're guarded in a secret place of memory,
Too much like visitations of the gods
To be mixed with everyday thinking.

8.

Before there was the tree, there was the house.
Before the house, the bed,
Before the bed, the quilt.

I could have stayed in the desert forever,
Except I was hungry, I had to eat.

So I returned to the house, I made a sandwich.
Don was in the kitchen; Claudia was reading on the deck.
A rabbit skittered once, then twice, then laid its ears against
    its head.

In the middle of the desert
You might be anyone,
Except you're never in the middle,
You're at the edge.

Then you're yourself again.
You look in the mirror,
It's like magic. There you are.

IV

HUNTINGTON MEADOW

Though I come from a long line of people intimate
With the bodies of horses,
Today, for the first time, I touched a horse.
I placed my hand on its left flank, just behind the shoulder.
The horse was standing beside me, eating grass.

I'm speaking here of things that come to feel essential
Though they happen at one moment in time.
You've never done it, then you've done it before, you're good at it.
You can't imagine your body without it.

Tanqueray up with an olive,
Nobody home, the brine
Still unexpected at the bottom of the glass.

When I touched the horse, I didn't move my hand.
The hide more skin than hair,
The muscle beneath it visceral, relaxed,
More like a lover's than a dog's.

Then, after I took my hand away, I immediately put it back.
The horse seemed all the while
Perfectly happy, ripping up grass at the roots.

That was the only sound, the sound
You hear when you're gardening, weeding the lawn,
Somebody right there beside you, also weeding,
Though because you lack nothing
You're also completely alone.

THE HUMMINGBIRD

Sunlight, food, and daily exercise produced
In me the body of an adult.
The attributes that made other adults attractive,
Though I was slow to acknowledge them, I recognized in myself.

I positioned myself in the morning light, just so.
I cruised the bottlebrush, birds-of-paradise,
And though I was still hungry
I came as close to the glass without touching as custom allows.

When you're ruled by your body, condemned
Each day to fill it so that tomorrow
You might fill it again,
Nothing is more erotic
Than a room without flowers.

In the *Phaedo*, after Socrates drinks the poison,
He walks around the house until his legs become heavy.
Then he lies down on his back.
He touches his feet,
Then touches his ankles, his shins.

When the cold has risen as far as his abdomen
He throws the sheet from his face.
Criton, he says, we owe a cock to Asclepios,
God of healing. Pay it without fail.

THE ACADEMY

Reluctantly, having returned to the very neighborhood
I'd once called home, I was staying at a small hotel.
I tied my tie, untied it, then tied it again.
I took the elevator to the lobby, exited
The revolving door, but the longer I walked

◆

The less attention I paid to detail.
The city's accretions, the shops, the people who frequented them,
No longer distracted me from the underlying contour of earth,
Which rose precipitously, then fell away,
So that just by walking forward, walking straight,

◆

Suddenly I saw for miles, and then,
Without adjusting my goal, saw only my feet.
One minute I stood at the edge of a great escarpment,
   overlooking the sea.
Then rocks I'd climbed gave way to a level plain,
There were fields of lavender, and in the distance

◆

What appeared to be a monastery perched at the top of a hill.
I took off my jacket, I loosened my tie;
I was anxious about getting lost.
But time had taught me only too well
The impossibility of attaining in the world

✦

The world I'd known, as Proust says in *The Past Recaptured*.
He's at the party at the house of the princess, it's been a long
  journey,
And he speaks of himself, unthinkingly,
As a young man, which makes everybody laugh.
When I arrived at the Academy at the top of the hill

✦

I found my place card, took my seat.
I ate the appetizer, then the main course, and like everyone
I endured the ceremony at which many names
Were called, including finally my own.
The phrase *a young man* is one my mother might have used,

✦

My mother for whom I was still always a child.
And if, as I heard my name, I registered certain changes
Which had taken place since childhood,
I judged them from the perspective she did,
One thing having followed another

✦

Unpredictably, but with purpose.

ONE LAST THING

This morning, which began like any morning,
My wife went running with the dog.
She tied her sneakers, secured the collar around his neck.

After they'd disappeared into the woods, the dog,
As was his habit, stopped to pee.
My wife looked off into the branches, which were laced with
    snow.
And though the leash was tight in her hand,
The collar fastened to the leash,
When she looked back the dog was gone.

How could she come home without the dog?
How could she explain not simply that he'd run away,
But that he'd vanished,
No shadow, no narrative,
A smudge of white against white snow?

Truthfully, I witnessed none of this.
But I can attest to the fact that when she returned,
The dog was trotting beside her.

No conclusions; observations.
I brewed the coffee, retrieved the paper from the stoop.
Without dislodging a single flake,
A cardinal settled on a branch.

THE HARBOR

1.

Slowly the harbor fills with fishing boats; the protagonist
Watches girls on the beach.
Every morning the same four girls, one with a bicycle.

The narrator explains that when you love one thing deeply, a
    person, a place,
Ultimately you love them all.
You know you're going to die, of course you do,
But you imagine a future, one that is a version of the past.
    What else could it be?

Your body, which since birth has served you well,
Continues to hold out its promise of both pleasure and pain.

Whom to prefer? The protagonist
Who understands nothing,
Or the narrator for whom everything is understood?

The slips stand empty, waiting for their boats.
The water follows the irregularities of the shoreline so a boat
    at sea,
Half hidden by the fishing shacks,
May seem to be sailing through the middle of town.

2.

How could it be possible? How could earth last longer than
    ourselves,
Who, feeling there was room
To store so many treasures,
Had thrown sea and sky repeatedly away?

Never did it occur to us that death, its first assault,
Might occur this very afternoon,
This afternoon whose schedule, hour by hour,
Has been settled in advance.

We have hesitated over which car to take, which service to call,
We are in the car, the whole day lies before us—

And we have no suspicion that death,
Which all along has been growing inside us,
Has chosen precisely this day to make its appearance,
Just as we're crossing Edgemere Drive.

3.

The protagonist prepares for bed, and having slept,
Awakens the following morning.
A force that once looked after him
Abandons him, a force of which he'd never been aware.

He tries to speak to that force.
He bargains, tries to give it a name.
He imagines what he'd say if, being dead, he heard his
    daughters' voices.

If you are speaking to me, he'd assure them,
I am listening to you speak. Who's listening now?

Which is more mysterious, more inexplicable, dying or
    staying alive?
Which makes more sense, each cell in your body
Servile, following orders,
Or a few now liberated not to care?

The protagonist prepares for bed;
He closes his book, then closes his eyes.

Boats in the harbor. A little boy
For whom he buys a dish of ice cream.

4.

It is in sickness that we recognize, no matter the circumstance,
  we're never alone.
That we are shackled to a body different from ourselves.

Before your mind existed, before it needed to exist, you were
  your body.
By taking care of it, your mother took care of you.
When by necessity your body was neglected, you learned to take
  care of yourself.

A body whom we have always known
But from whom we are worlds apart.

You wanted to be neglected;
You needed to invent your mind.

A body who has no knowledge of us,
Though he causes us pain.
A body to whom it is impossible to make ourselves understood.

In the mind, you're capable of soothing yourself
Not only when you're neglected, but when you're loved.

5.

Evenings, whenever I watched my daughters sleep, I felt like
    an angel.
I'd never seen an angel, but that's how I felt.

Immediately they smiled in the morning, but sometimes
    they cried;
I'd hold their tiny bodies against me.
Why are you crying? They couldn't say.

When I woke up from surgery,
I could open only one eye.
I could hear voices, but I couldn't see.
Come over here, I asked, so I can see you. Then I saw.

The Temple of Baal is gone forever,
Likewise the great stone Buddhas of Bamiyan.
Titian's *Battle of Spoleto*, Caravaggio's *Saint John*—all of
    them gone.

Often I'm asked if I'd return to where I came from,
Resume the life of the person I once was,
But the answer, any answer,
Implies a narrative
About the purpose of suffering.

6.

In the back of the closet is a suitcase filled with clothes.
Look how carefully the shirts have been folded,
How lovingly the handkerchiefs have been pressed,
Handkerchiefs that never dried an eye.

He might have wished for another season, longer or later, winter
    or summer,
It wouldn't matter which.
Hasn't he worked hard, harder than anyone?

The boats come in, the boats go out.
The docks are paved with starfish, which the fishermen discard.

Can there be any day but this?
Look, there is the sea, and there is the sky.

PASTORAL

Every morning people do exactly what I do.
They make their beds, they practice their lutes.
Then why am I so afraid?

Girls are stringing daisies,
Rearranging peaches in a china bowl.
Boys are sulking in the forest, thinking about death.

But after they've swept the cave,
Tidied up the pallet of rumpled ferns,
Out come the lutes, they play.
The birds begin to sing.

The girls are waiting
In the gallery, braiding ribbons
In each other's hair. Where are the boys?

I know it's been the longest year on record.
Our crutches are worn out.
For everyone, it's been the same.

But you know how this ends as well as I do.
The lutes come out,
The birds begin to sing,
The boys and girls are lying in the grass. If anything

Earth looks a little younger now.
I love you, earth.
What space I inhabit
You'll fill with water or sky.

ACKNOWLEDGMENTS

GRATEFUL ACKNOWLEDGMENT is made to the editors of the following magazines, in which these poems first appeared:

The Atlantic: "Hotel Earth"
Brink: "Stars," "Two and a Half Odes"
The Colorado Review: "The Interpreter"
The Courtland Review: "Dorsoduro"
Literary Imagination: "Seafarer"
Smartish Pace: "We Can Say"
The Threepenny Review: "Now and Then," reprinted on
    Poetry Daily

"Two People," from *Forever*, initially published in *Adroit Journal*, appears in the 2024 Pushcart Prize Anthology.

"Now and Then" also adapts phrases from Donne's *Devotions*, Ruskin's *Praeterita*, and Bassani's *In rima e senza*; "We Can Say" from the Ulysses canto of the *Inferno*, Langdon Hammer's *James Merrill*, and Gaia Pianigiani's *New York Times* essays; "The Interpreter" from Natasha Trethewey's "Goodbye to a Symbol" and Proust's *Contre Saint-Beuve*. Like "Seafarer," the first part of "After Dinner" is translated loosely from the Old English.